Ref 1203
Amnesty International - Rachel - Balham 11.97. 50p

TARTANWARE

PRINCESS IRA VON FURSTENBERG

TARTANWARE

SOUVENIRS FROM SCOTLAND

with Andrew Nicolls

PAVILION

First published in Great Britain in 1996 by
PAVILION BOOKS LIMITED
26 Upper Ground, London SE1 9PD

Designed by Bernard Higton

A CIP catalogue record for this book is available
from the British Library.

ISBN 1 85793 514 4

Text set in Simoncini Garamond
Printed and bound in Spain by Bookprint

2 4 6 8 10 9 7 5 3 1

This book can be ordered direct from the publisher.
Please contact the Marketing Department.
But try your bookshop first.

CONTENTS

FOREWORD

MY passion for tartanware began, like many such fascinations, quite by chance. Some years ago, while browsing through the antique stalls lining London's Portobello Road, a vitrine full of delightful objects caught my eye. The little items on show ranged from snuff boxes to photograph frames, but what made the display so distinctive was that each object was beautifully decorated in tartan. Utterly entranced, I was unable to resist buying a couple of these gaily coloured pieces, the first acquisitions of what would eventually grow into an extensive collection.

I soon discovered that the objects which I had chanced upon were examples of what is collectively known as tartanware. Decorative souvenirs made in Scotland in the latter part of the nineteenth century, tartanware is, more precisely, just one variety of a range of goods known as Mauchlineware, after the Ayrshire town where the trade was originally based. For about fifty years from the middle of the nineteenth century onwards, thousands of such pieces were produced, capitalizing on the immense contemporary popularity of Scotland as a holiday destination and supplying countless Victorian tourists with charming mementoes of their visits.

Since that Saturday morning excursion to the Portobello Road, I have found hundreds of different examples of tartanware but, most extraordinarily, I have never found two pieces that are identical. This just goes to show in what great numbers these souvenirs must have been made. Many of my discoveries are objects that might have been used in Victorian households, and the picture they provide of the activities of a bygone era only adds to their appeal. The greater number of items in my collection, however, comprise pieces which are unlikely ever to have been used by anyone, at least in the way in which they were first intended. A thread spool encased in a tartan-decorated egg is hardly the most practical tool for a hard-working seamstress – yet somehow this does not lessen its attraction.

Collectors like to specialize, and I am no exception. My collection of tartan-ware focuses, although not exclusively, on household articles and knitting and sewing accessories, items which I particularly enjoy for their stunning diversity. More recently, I have found much larger pieces decorated in tartan, including side tables and tea caddies. I never cease to be amazed by the enchanting and ingenious way in which tartan has been used to enliven the appearance of objects for everyday use.

One of the greatest joys of collecting remains the thrill of the unexpected discovery. A few years ago, I mentioned to a French friend that I was interested in tartanware. She inquired what it looked like and, after I had explained the objects to her, she suddenly perked up and declared that she might have some examples of what I was describing in a box downstairs. The items in question had been bequeathed to her by an old aunt and she had simply set them to one side without ever giving them a moment's thought. There, tucked away on top of a shelf, lay a treasure trove of nearly forty tartanware pieces.

It may seem odd that someone with Italian and Austro-Hungarian parents should be so fascinated with Scottish antiquities. I suppose that my great-grand-parents, the Duke and Duchess of Hamilton, must have left a small part of their Scottish heritage in me. If you find tartan irresistible, as I do, I hope this book will enable you to share the enjoyment I have gained over the years from these delightful and intriguing pieces.

Princess Ira von Furstenberg

THE TARTAN PHENOMENON

THERE is nothing more quintessentially Scottish than tartan. As instantly recognizable as a flag, this family of colourful chequered patterns vividly evokes the culture of the country, its history and its people. How tartan came to be one of the most effective of all national symbols is a fascinating, complex story.

Tartan's history is surprisingly rife with controversy. Distinguishing fact from fiction, myth from reality, has proved something of a difficult task for historians; the scanty evidence which survives of tartan's origins has provoked lively and often fierce debate. Tartan, as it is popularly conceived today, is the insignia of clan identity or membership. But the process by which this humble woven pattern became the emblem, not only of Scottish clans, but of Scotland itself, is by no means straightforward.

Tartan is undoubtedly ancient. From Roman sources, particularly the writings of Virgil, we know that the Celts were noted for their colourful striped clothing. A fragment of chequered cloth in natural light and dark wool, dating from the third century AD, exhibits at least some of the characteristics we identify with tartan today. Known as the 'Falkirk Tartan', this ancient weave is now in the Royal Museum of Scotland, Edinburgh. On the basis of rather less hard evidence, many tartan enthusiasts over the years have been tempted to claim that a system of clan tartans can be traced back to the dawn of Scottish history. However appealing this view may be, there is no historical fact to support it.

The earliest known documentation of the existence of tartan, dating from 1538, can be found in the accounts of the treasurer to King James V: 'for iij elnes Helande Tertane to be hoiss to the Kingis Grace...' The term 'Helande' is of special significance: tartan, however and whenever it originated, is first and foremost the native twill weave of the Highlands.

The Highlands have long been shrouded in mystery, myth and romance. Geologically separated from the Lowlands and Borders by the Highland Boundary Fault, which runs roughly from Helensburgh on the Firth of Clyde to Stonehaven on the northeast coast, the Highlands are no less culturally distinct from the rest of Scotland than they are geographically. This wild rugged land-scape with its heather-clad slopes, steep mountains and deep glens was settled by the Picts, descendants of the ancient Celts who first arrived in Britain in the seventh century BC. Over the centuries the various tribes scattered the length and breadth of the Highlands, together with later incomers such as the Scotti (literally 'bandits') from Northern Ireland, and began to merge to form large tribal groups.

By the fourteenth century AD, the Highland clan was beginning to appear in a recognizable form. Unlike the Lowlanders, who had adopted the feudal system introduced by the Normans, Highlanders held their land as a clan, with each clan voting for its chief and owing allegiance to him. Clan members were often, but not exclusively, related, the 'Mac' prefix of many Scottish names meaning 'son of'. Clans tended to be based in a particular district, with land leased out to smallholders under the jurisdiction of the chief. While the Lowlands gradually became Anglicized, the Highlands remained Gaelic-speaking. The Highland identity, with its Gaelic tongue and clan system, eventually came to be expressed in a distinctive form of dress.

Accounts written by early travellers to the Highlands provide a picture of typical Highland dress around the beginning of the seventeenth century. John Taylor, an early English visitor, wrote in 1618:

'Their habit is shoos with but one sole apiece; stockings (which they call short hose) made of a warm stuffe of divers colours, which they call Tartane; as for breeches, many of them, nor their forefathers, never wore any, but a jerkin of the same stuff that their hose is of, their garters being bands or wreaths of hay or straw, with a plead about their shoulders, which is a mantle of divers colours, much finer and lighter stuff than their hose, with flat blue caps on their head, a handkerchiefe knit with two knots about their necke...'

The belted plaid, or 'feileadh', of the Highlander was a long, wide piece of woven cloth, pleated and belted at the waist and secured at the shoulder with a brooch. This warm outer garment served as a cloak, blanket or makeshift bedding. There are even more dramatic stories of Highlanders caught abroad on winter nights surviving the freezing temperatures by wrapping themselves in dampened feileadhs. If such stories are true, the ice-encrusted cloak must have acted rather like a snow hole, cocooning the stranded traveller and minimizing the loss of precious body heat.

The feileadh was worn over a long saffron-coloured shirt and tartan hose; later over a tartan jerkin and trews. There was no attempt to coordinate tartan garments, and different tartans were worn together. By the eighteenth century a short version of the long, belted plaid had evolved: the feileadh beg, philibeg or filibeg. This early form of kilt might be worn in battle or in other circumstances where greater freedom of movement was required. The sporran or 'spleuchan', a small goatskin purse initially worn at the waist, also dates from this later period.

Women wore the tonnag, a small tartan shawl, over the shoulders and the arisaid, a length of pleated woven fabric, secured at the breast with a brooch and belted at the waist. The arisaid served the same practical purpose as the feileadh. Early forms were simply striped, like the homespun blankets from which they derived, but the typical arisaid pattern evolved as a 'white plaid', in other words a chequered design over a white or pale ground.

A LADY AND GENTLEMAN IN HEBRIDEAN DRESS

The innate Celtic love of colour was expressed in the vivid shades of tartan. Relying on natural dyes from native plants, Highland dyers could achieve bright red, yellow, dark blue and green, all strong clear colours that served to create harmonious plaids. Natural colours were intrinsically softer than the harsh chemical dyes which supplanted them after industrialization, but they were not necessarily muted or subdued. One early reference, dating from 1582, makes it clear that the duller colours may have been favoured for the purposes of camouflage:

'Their ancestors wore plaids of many different colours and numbers still retain this custom, but the majority, now, in their dress, prefer a dark brown, imitating nearly the leaves of the heather, that when lying upon the heath in the day, they may not be discovered by the appearance of their clothes...'

There is at least some evidence that certain tartans or plaids were associated with certain districts. *A Description of the Western Isles of Scotland* written by Martin Martin in 1695 includes the following passage:

'Each Isle differs from the other in their fancy of making Plads, as to the Stripes in Breadth and Colours. This Humour is as different thro the main Land of the Highlands, in-so-far that they who have seen these Places, are able, at the first view of a Man's Plad, to guess the Place of his Residence...'

This association of pattern with locality may have had something to do with which natural dyestuffs were available in a particular region, or, more likely, with the traditions preserved by local village weavers, handing their skills down from one generation to the next. Since the clan system meant that people living in the same district generally belonged to the same clan, the 'clan tartan' probably had its roots in these simple conjunctions. Given that a clan might be dispersed over a fairly large area, however, the relationship between tartans and districts must have been fairly tenuous. No amount of fanciful conjecture can provide any hard evidence of specific tartan 'setts' (as patterns are known) being ascribed to particular clans before the start of the eighteenth century.

As the centuries progressed, the proud and independent Highland clans had become notorious for their savagery and general barbarism. Outside the Highlands, the sight of the tartan or 'mountain habit' was a cause for alarm. Swooping down from their mountain strongholds, the 'tartan hordes' terrorized their Lowland neighbours, raiding farms, stealing cattle and extorting protection money. The Macgregor clan was a byword for lawlessness; after one outrage in 1603 a law was passed which decreed that anyone going about under the Macgregor name could be put to death on sight. The surviving members of the clan, in hiding in remote mountain areas, earned themselves the nickname 'The Children of the Mist' for their ability to melt from sight. Rob Roy, the Highland Robin Hood of Sir Walter Scott's romance, was a Macgregor.

Clans were no more peaceable amongst themselves. Feuds and power struggles over territory and supremacy made for a bloody history. The Macgregors' chief rivals, the Campbells, were noted for their scheming opportunism; their instinctive ability to back the winning side enabled the 'men of the twisted mouths' to rise to become one of the most powerful of all the clans. When

ROB ROY AND THE BAILLIE, 1886

William III sought to subdue the troublesome Highlands by enforcing an official oath of allegiance, the Campbells earned the lasting enmity of every other Highland clan for their treacherous role in the 1692 massacre at Glencoe. Billeted with the Macdonalds for over a fortnight in the depths of February, Campbell troops secretly acting on behalf of the government turned on their hosts and murdered the chief and thirty-seven other clansmen, women and children. Glencoe did little but strengthen the innate Highland distrust of authority and prepare the way for the Jacobite risings of 1715 and 1745.

PRINCE CHARLES EDWARD STUART IN EDINBURGH, 1745

Tartans probably first began to become specific to particular clans as a result of military requirements. Uniform battledress has always had both practical and morale-boosting advantages, and where regiments were raised by clan chiefs from the ranks of their clansmen, it made sense for soldiers to adopt the tartan of their leader. One of the first such recorded instances dates from 1703 when the Laird of Grant ordered his men to turn out in coats, trews and hose of the same tartan, in effect in livery. It is likely that other clan militia were similarly instructed. Away from the battlefield, however, tartans remained as various as ever. Contemporary portraits rarely show any consistency in the tartans worn by their sitters.

With the rise of nationalist spirit following the much-hated Act of Union in 1707, tartans grew brighter and more striking, proclaiming the wearer's loyalty to the exiled James VII of Scotland and II of England: the 'king over the water'. During the first Jacobite rising of 1715, Highlanders discontented with the Union rallied to the Stuart cause. At the battle of Sheriffmuir, near Stirling, the Jacobite forces led by the Earl of Mar numbered some 12,000 clansmen; nevertheless they were unable to defeat a much smaller pro-government force under Argyll and had to retreat. A contemporary account of the battle gives a vivid picture of Highlanders in battle:

'[The Highlanders'] cloaths are composed of two short vests, the one above reaching only to their waste, the other about six inches longer, short stockings which reaches not quite to their knee and no breetches; but above all they have another piece of the same stuff, of about six yards long which they tie about them in such a manner that it covers their thighs and all their body when they please, but commonly it's fixed on their left shoulder, and leaves their right arm free. This kind of mantell they throw away when they are ready to engage, to be lighter and less encumber'd, and if they are beat it remains in the field, as happened to our left wing, who having lost that part of their cloaths which protects them most from the cold and which likewise serves them for bedcloaths, could not resist the violent cold of the season...'

The second Jacobite rising of 1745 was led by Prince Charles Edward, 'Bonnie Prince Charlie', the son of the Old Pretender. The campaign was disastrous from the start and culminated in the final crushing defeat of the rebel forces at Culloden in 1746. The 'Young Pretender' was forced to flee for his life and spent months evading capture hiding in the Highlands. With his eventual escape, 'safely o'er the friendly main', in the words of the haunting popular

MALCOLM MCPHERSON, CORPORAL
IN THE HIGHLAND REGIMENT

song, the hopes of his supporters dwindled and died. It was the beginning of the end for the Highland clan system.

During the '45, tartan had become a potent symbol of nationalist aspirations. One tartan, the Huntly, was evidently worn over a wide area and by a number of different families as a sign of a shared Jacobite sympathy. Prince Charles Edward received many gifts of plaids and is said to have worn the tartans of the clans with whom he stayed in his journeys about the Highlands. Much of the memorabilia cherished by the Prince's supporters long after his departure consists of tartan fragments from garments he is supposed to have worn.

Despite the fact that tartan had been worn by men fighting on both sides at Culloden, it had become sufficiently identified with anti-Union fervour for the government to view its prohibition as an effective means of striking at the heart of clan identity. Accordingly, the wearing of Highland dress of any description was banned. The so-called 'Proscription' stated:

'...no man or boy within that part of Great Britain called Scotland, other than such as shall be employed as Officers or Soldiers in His Majesty's Forces, shall on any pretext whatsoever wear or put on the clothes commonly called Highland clothes (that is to say) the Plaid, Philabeg, or little Kilt, Trowse, Shoulder belts or any part whatsoever of what peculiarly belongs to the Highland Garb; and that no tartan or Part-coloured plaid or stuff shall be used for Great Coats, or upper Coats...'

The penalty was six months' imprisonment for a first offence, transportation for a second. Despite pleas that the Highland dress was a practical necessity, given the harsh conditions of climate and terrain, the ban remained in force for thirty-eight years. Memories of the Proscription are enshrined in such landmarks as the 'Bridge of Trousers' or Tig an Tuish, linking the Isle of Seil with Argyll, the territory of the Campbells. Those crossing from island to mainland supposedly exchanged the kilt for trousers at the halfway point.

The Proscription did not apply to the Scottish armed forces in the service of the Crown. Scottish regiments defending British colonies in distant parts of the globe were permitted to retain their traditional tartan dress, which proved an incentive to recruitment. The Black Watch military tartan is thought to have originated sometime during the latter part of the eighteenth century.

After the '45, the lands of the rebels were confiscated and the powers of the clan chieftains strictly limited. The economic structure of the Highlands began to change. From about the middle of the eighteenth century to the middle of the nineteenth, the Highlands steadily and surely depopulated, as landlords evicted tenants to make way for sheep, and poor crofters looked for better lives in the New World. Tartan production shifted away from the Highland villages to new workshops and factories in towns bordering Lowland areas. Tartan, the uniform of the Scottish regiments and always a durable and cheap material, was also supplied in great quantities to clothe slaves in colonial outposts.

Paradoxically, the seeds of the great tartan revival were sown at this singularly low point in its history. The Highland regiments acquitted themselves well in the Seven Years War and the American War of Independence, and later during subsequent campaigns against the French. The Highlander, once the feared barbarian, gradually began to acquire a reputation for honour and bravery.

GEORGE IV
IN HIGHLAND DRESS

In the late eighteenth century Scottish officers based in London formed a Highland Society, which celebrated every aspect of Highland culture and proved instrumental in achieving the eventual repeal of the Proscription in 1782. Once more, Highlanders could wear their native dress without sanction, although contemporary accounts make it clear that over the years many had simply defied the ban in any case. After the repeal of the Proscription, the Highland Society also made some attempt to trace, record and verify the old tartan setts.

Sir Walter Scott (1771–1832), the 'Wizard of the North', played a pivotal role in the rehabilitation of the Highland reputation. In Scott's Waverley novels, a history marked by barbarism and bloody conflict was transformed into stirring adventure, and Highland clans and customs were sympathetically and engagingly portrayed. The image of the Highlands as a romantic wilderness began to take hold of the popular imagination.

In 1822 Scott, a supreme showman, helped to stage the epoch-making visit of George IV to Scotland. The event was a tumultuous success. The corpulent King, the first reigning monarch to visit the country for nearly two centuries, entranced his Scottish subjects by announcing his intention of wearing the kilt, and duly appeared at a levee clad in the Royal Stuart tartan with the modest addition of pink tights underneath.

Following the King's lead, Highlander and Lowlander alike rushed to order quantities of tartan. The weaving industry was quick to respond: manufacturers shrewdly promoted the notion that each Highland clan or Lowland family should be distinguished by its own tartan. Naturally enough, during the years of the Proscription, many of the old setts had lapsed into obscurity. More often than not, the clan tartans now eagerly adopted by Scottish families were simply stock tartans which had been furnished with a ready-made history and identity. Many of these were much more colourful and lively than earlier versions and dated back no further than the lifting of the Proscription.

The clan tartan idea was a godsend for tartan manufacturers, whose military and colonial markets were fast dwindling. Tartans, which had once largely been distinguished only by numbers in pattern books, began to acquire names, not only of clans, but of districts, cities and even famous military victories. Over two thousand years after the first length of tartan cloth was woven, the 'clan tartan' had officially arrived.

One of the strangest episodes in tartan's convoluted history occurred in 1842 with the publication of *Vestiarium Scoticum* ('The Scottish Wardrobe'). The book, purportedly a copy of a sixteenth-century manuscript, described seventy-two clan tartans and thus appeared to provide historical evidence of the antiquity of the clan tartan idea. Some of the tartans were ascribed to Lowland families, although tartan had never before been associated with any region outside the Highlands.

The book was the work of two brothers, John Sobieski Stuart and Charles Edward Stuart, who were widely believed to be the grandsons of Bonnie Prince Charlie and did little to dispel the notion. By the time of the book's publication, the 'Sobieski' brothers, who began life more prosaically as John and Charles

QUEEN VICTORIA ON HORSEBACK WITH JOHN BROWN

Allen, had been circulating some of the patterns from the manuscript for nearly twenty years. The published work was widely accepted as valid and featured illustrations achieved by means of the 'Machine Painting' process invented by William and Andrew Smith of Mauchline, who were to figure so prominently in the development of tartanware. Like the Sobieskis' ancestry, the manuscript was undoubtedly a fake, but its appearance at this time indicates the depth of interest in the clan tartan idea.

The wider identification of tartan with Scottishness owes much to the influence of Queen Victoria. The young Queen, only two years married, made her first visit to Scotland in September 1842 and was immediately enchanted with the Highlands, its scenery, its people and its tartans. Prince Albert thought the landscape reminiscent of Germany and much enjoyed the shooting. Two years later the royal couple returned and their affection for 'the dear, dear Highlands' deepened. They set about looking for a permanent Scottish residence.

'A pretty little castle in the old Scottish style', Balmoral was to prove the most beloved of all the Queen's homes. Victoria and Albert first stayed at Balmoral in 1848, and bought it two years later. In place of the old house, Albert commissioned a new, much larger castle in the 'Scottish Baronial' style to accommodate the royal entourage.

Victoria and Albert expressed their devotion to the Highlands by adopting tartan with a fervour. Balmoral was furnished with tartan curtains, tartan upholstery and tartan carpets. Albert and the Royal children wore the kilt; Victoria often sported a tartan sash. Albert designed a special Balmoral tartan, which was worn by all members of the Royal household. The Royal Family attended the Braemar Gathering and Highland Games, learned Scottish dancing and developed an affection for the bagpipes.

Where the Royal Family led, others followed. By the 1860s, the Highlands were becoming a popular destination for tourists from the south, coming to enjoy the sport or simply to gaze at the landscape. Aristocrats and wealthy industrialists began to buy up Scottish estates or establish game lodges for the shooting season. The railway from Perth to Inverness was completed in 1863, bringing more and more visitors into the heart of the Highlands.

The happy life at Balmoral came to an abrupt end with the sudden death of Prince Albert in 1861. Queen Victoria, prostrate with grief, went into virtual seclusion for more than a decade. During the long years of her mourning, she came to rely more and more on the counsel and support of her loyal Highland ghillie, John Brown, a dependence that caused some consternation in official circles and a mild public scandal. Brown died in 1883, but the Queen's affection for the Highlands never wavered and she returned there year after year until her death.

The enthusiasm with which Victoria embraced the Highland tartans has proved utterly infectious. Tartans continue to be created at a great rate and today there are over two thousand setts officially listed. There are dress tartans for formal occasions and hunting tartans for sport, district tartans, chiefs' tartans and royal tartans, 'modern' and 'ancient' tartans and, of course, clan tartans by the hundreds.

The tartan phenomenon shows no sign of abating. As *haute couture* or street fashion, tartan is worn all over the world by people without a drop of Scottish blood in their veins. Tartan decorates everything from biscuit tins to sofas in smart drawing rooms; it lends its innate festivity to Christmas ribbon, wrapping paper and baubles. From its origins as the practical garb of a mountain people, tartan has become an international trend. It is amusing to speculate what the clansmen of old would have made of it all.

THE QUEEN'S BEDROOM AT BALMORAL

THE HISTORY OF TARTANWARE

T‌ARTANWARE owes its origin to the inveterate eighteenth-century habit of taking snuff. Tartan-clad objects first appeared in the form of snuff boxes around the turn of the nineteenth century. Fifty years later, the tartanware trade had expanded to encompass a huge variety of diverse household articles and souvenirs marketed throughout England and Scotland as 'Scotch Goods'.

The Scottish have long prided themselves on the manufacture of high-quality woodware. In the latter part of the eighteenth century, the native skills of carving, turning and shaping wood found particular expression in the form of snuff boxes. What made the Scottish snuff box unique was the wooden or 'hidden' hinge, an integral constructional feature composed of interlocking segments of the box lid and back. It is important for snuff to be kept dry. Wooden boxes fitted with metal hinges will not remain airtight for long, since metal is unable to change shape in response to atmospheric conditions, as wood does. The invention of the wooden hinge proved the foundation of the Scottish snuff-box making industry.

Who actually perfected the wooden hinge is a matter of debate. Some attribute the invention to a certain John Sandy of Alyth, Perthshire, an unfortunate invalid who worked at his trade from his bed and was rather susceptible to strong drink. Others maintain that it was Charles Stiven, a joiner working around the same time, who first devised the wooden hinge.

In 1783, Stiven set up as a snuff-box maker in an old stagecoach booking office in Laurencekirk, Kincardineshire, probably under the patronage of his former employer Lord Gardenstone, who was a local landowner and enthusiastic

snuff-taker himself. Whether Stiven actually developed the wooden hinge or simply bought the secret from Sandy, he proceeded to flourish in his trade.

Stiven recognized, like other early makers, that a plain wooden snuff box, while eminently practical, was hardly an object of beauty. With tartan sides and a Scottish scene hand-painted on the lid, however, it became a desirable addition to a snuff-taker's collection. Stiven employed two artists to paint his boxes. The tartan decoration was applied directly to the wood, and the lid was enriched with pictures of Scottish landscapes, castles, portraits of Robert Burns or hunting scenes, all skilfully executed in paint or pen and ink. These 'drawn tartan' pieces, now extremely rare, exhibit the finest degree of craftsmanship.

The secret of the hidden hinge did not remain secret for long. By the 1820s, there were as many as fifty Scottish snuff-box manufacturers, and the centre of production had shifted southwards to Ayrshire. Demand for these beautifully crafted artefacts was high. The price paid for a box of the finest quality soared

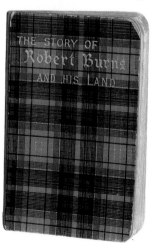

to seven pounds, while the industry as a whole is said to have generated an astonishing total of £6,000 worth of revenue in 1825 alone. Charles Stiven and Sons, the leading firm in the field, was eventually awarded a Royal Warrant and invited to contribute to the Royal Collection at Balmoral.

Just as the trade reached its height, snuffing began to go out of fashion. Over the next decade and a half from the mid-1820s onwards, the snuff-box making business slowly sank into decline; although snuff boxes continued to be made in Scotland right through to the 1870s, demand shrank to a fraction of its former level. By the middle of the century, most of the original firms had ceased to trade.

A few far-sighted individuals, however, had spotted the potential in the growing market for souvenirs, as Scotland began to emerge as a popular holiday destination for Victorian tourists. Souvenirs, of course, must be affordable and the search began for cheaper ways of decorating than hand labour. Instead of snuff boxes, the manufacture expanded to include tea caddies and boxes for many other purposes.

The firm which was to become most closely identified with tartanware was established in 1810 by John and James Smith in Mauchline, Ayrshire, a town otherwise known for its connection with Robert Burns. Under the direction of brothers William (1795–1847?) and Andrew Smith (1797–1869), the firm's original emphasis began to shift away from the production of finely crafted pieces to cheaper decorative goods. Collectively known as Mauchlineware, these souvenirs were eventually produced in a variety of forms, encompassing product lines decorated with transfers, ferns, photographs and tartan.

Sycamore was the favoured wood for Mauchlineware products. As a close-grained hardwood, it was ideal both for fashioning small intricate items and for constructing wooden hinges; its light tone also provided a good ground for decoration and a pleasing mellow colour when varnished.

An early development was transferware, which imitated the effect of the old hand-decorated snuff boxes. Printed transfers of scenic views taken from engraved plates were applied to sycamore boxes; layers of varnish created a warm, glowing finish. The first transfers used by the Smiths were of the highest quality and the effect was nearly indistinguishable from the old pen and ink decoration, although much less difficult and far cheaper to produce.

Mechanizing tartan decoration presented considerably greater difficulty. In those days, long before the development of reliable and accurate colour reproduction processes, coloured decoration generally meant laborious and expensive hand labour. The first Mauchline tartanware was produced by printing directly onto the wood, but this crude technique cannot have resulted in anything like a true representation of tartan.

By the 1840s the ingenious Smiths had developed a method for printing tartan onto paper. The printed paper was pasted onto the wooden object, the joins painted black, and gilt and varnish applied on top. With careful application, it was difficult to tell the difference between hand-painted and transfer-printed pieces.

The technique which the Smiths invented, 'Machine Painting', involved the use of a sliding row of pens, which marked a sheet of black paper with thin ruled lines of colour. Each tartan colour was applied in turn, working from the lighter to the darker shades. Bands of colour in the correct distribution were achieved by lifting up the pens which were not required, and shifting the entire row across to fill in the stripes line by line. The paper was then turned and the process repeated to create the chequered effect of tartan. One of the advantages of the technique was that it could be used on leather and wood as well as on paper.

The machine painting process was used to create the illustrations for the Sobieskis' *Vestiarium Scoticum* in 1842. Eight years later, the Smiths adopted the same method to illustrate their own work, *Authenticated Tartans of the Clans and Families of Scotland*, a compilation of sixty-nine tartans which they researched from a variety of sources, consulting tartan merchants, historians and clan chiefs to validate the setts. As shrewd as they were innovative, the Smiths were not slow to see the potential of the clan tartan idea as a means of promoting and establishing their own tartanware business.

Tartanware took off. From the middle of the century onwards, vast quantities of inexpensive souvenirs were produced with an incredible diversity of decoration and design. A significant proportion of these objects were sewing accessories, but there were also many different kinds of boxes, for keeping anything from stamps to pen nibs, as well as a host of other practical artefacts. The tartans themselves ranged from clan tartans to simple chequered designs with no true pedigree. In the case of more authentic decoration, the name of the tartan might be stamped on the piece.

The Smiths prospered with the expansion of the trade. During the latter part of the century, the 'Box Works', their factory, employed some four hundred people in and around Mauchline, and the firm even had a warehouse and shop in Birmingham. Their chief rivals in the production of tartanware was another large Mauchline manufacturer, Davidson, Wilson and Amphlet, who employed around three hundred people. The majority of the tartanware workforce comprised young boys, who worked at home coating the pieces with varnish.

The glossy lacquered finish typical of tartanware objects was achieved by the laborious application of up to thirty-six coats.

As time went by and production levels increased, the quality of the goods began to suffer. Instead of wood, some tartanware was made in cheaper materials such as papier mâché. After a fire destroyed Smiths' tartan printing machine, cheaper transfers bought in from other manufacturers were used instead, but these lacked the clarity and precision of the early examples. By the end of the century, standards were fairly low. The tartan cladding was shoddily made and poorly applied, so that seams rarely matched up. At the same time, the appeal of Scotland as a holiday destination was waning and the demand for souvenirs began to tail off. When another fire destroyed Smiths' factory in 1933, decades of slow decline came to a full stop.

The rediscovery of tartanware by modern collectors has brought to light a fascinating and long-neglected industry. As the popularity of these collectables grows, they are inevitably commanding higher prices and the better pieces can now fetch quite surprising amounts of money. Once simply dismissed as bric-à-brac or emphemera, tartanware is now prized for its craftsmanship and for the beauty of its decoration. As with any other field of collecting, the value of a piece reflects its age, rarity and condition. Hand-decorated examples, naturally enough, are more sought-after than the later transfer-printed pieces. Nevertheless, it is still possible to find affordable examples of tartanware in markets and antique shops not only in Britain, but also in Europe, North America, South Africa and Australia. In tartanware's heyday, these charming mementoes of Scotland were exported all over the world, and the international appeal of tartan today must owe something to the success of this curious and lively trade, which flourished in Ayrshire for over seventy years.

THE
TARTANWARE

TARTAN FOR A SEAMSTRESS

An enormous number of tartanware objects were created with knitting, sewing or needlework in mind. This is far from surprising, since Victorian ladies passed many an evening engaged in the gentle art of embroidery. Skill with the needle was a prized accomplishment. Young girls learned a repertoire of stitches at their mother's knee, practising their techniques and, as often as not, their letters, by working samplers featuring names, dates, mottoes and alphabets. Antimacassars, doilies, cushions, seat covers, table linen and other accessories provided plenty of scope for the expression of the needlewoman's skill, as did embroidered detail on frocks and trimmings on Sunday bonnets. After the introduction of aniline dyes in the middle of the nineteenth century, a wide range of brightly coloured wools and silks was available to the seamstress, and needlepoint or 'Berlin woolwork' pictures were all the rage.

Tartanware, aside from its fashionable association with Scotland, could not help but appeal to the Victorian love of pattern and decorative richness. There was another factor in its favour. Victorians at home took pains to disguise the utility of practical objects in everyday use. A tartanware thread shuttle or wool container transformed a working tool into a decorative object worthy of display in the drawing room or boudoir.

Three miniature sewing accessories display the wit and ingenuity of tartanware (right). The little barrel, only two inches high, is decorated with the popular Prince Charlie tartan. It splits in the middle to reveal a cylindrical compartment for storing needles. The three-quarter egg, decked in the McFarlane tartan, has an ivory knob for lifting the cover from its base. Inside is a round needle container. The dainty little heart pin-cushion, featuring the Stuart tartan, is not the most practical of objects, as only a limited number of pins can be pushed in at the side, between the tartan covers.

This object, shaped like a curling stone, is in fact a thread-dispenser (left). Inside the McLean tartan container are six prongs for thread spools, each thread being drawn out through the holes on the circumference of the piece. In Victorian times, threads were manufactured in different widths or gauges, with the most common being 40, 50 and 60. This sewing accessory features two holes for each of these gauges.

Sewing accessories came in all shapes and sizes. This red and black checked miniature beer barrel on its black stand serves as a dispenser of string. The object separates in the middle to allow a ball of string to be placed inside, with the end threaded through the imitation tap. A small quantity of tartanware featured simple checked patterns rather than recognizable tartans. The egg was a favourite shape of tartanware manufacturers. Many different egg-shaped objects in a range of sizes were produced to house a variety of items. This Stuart egg, on its black base, holds a thimble. The scalloped box, decorated in the rare McLachlan tartan, opens to reveal four thread spools, a thimble and a needle case. Each thread is fed through a separate hole to prevent the kind of hopeless tangles that lurk in the bottom of many a sewing basket.

A delightful example of early tartanware, this flask-shaped piece shows how everyday articles could be packaged in an attractive and amusing way. Only two inches high, the flask splits in the middle to reveal a thread spool fitted onto a little rod with a thimble perched on top. In many similar designs, the central rod is hollow and serves as a needle container. An astonishing number of tartanware containers for sewing accessories are in the form of miniature flasks and barrels – perhaps in a lighthearted reference to Scotland's other great export!

Gaily decorated thread or silk winders in a variety of shapes make eye-catching accessories for the needle-woman. Many hundreds of tartanware sewing accessories were produced, from needle cases to thimble holders and wool containers. There are probably fifty different types of thread winder alone, some of which also served as pin cushions. Each object can be found in a range of different shapes, sizes and, of course, tartans – a wealth of variations on a theme, which makes tartanware collecting so intriguing. The lower two cross-shaped winders are decorated respectively in Caledonia and Forbes, while the traditionally styled winder on the top left is decked in Rob Roy.

C lad in McDuff tartan, this V-shaped object is actually a scissors box. The interior is subdivided into three compartments of varying size to accommodate graduated pairs of scissors. The compartments themselves are luxuriously lined in blue velvet, so as not to blunt the blades, and the inner lid is lined in matching blue silk. The box is fastened with a decorated clasp – all in all, a treasure for a seamstress.

Many thread manufacturers sold their wares packaged in tartanware containers; the example on the left features the name of Clark and Co. of Paisley, a well-known firm. Thread holes inset in the sides or tops of boxes were made of bone or ivory. The round boxes on the right, which may have been used for storing wool or string, are designed to look like drums, with gold coachlines imitating the effect of rope. The boxes feature the Macpherson tartan, offset by a simple green plaid.

THE HIGHLAND KITCHEN

Few places in the home escaped the attention of the tartan enthusiast. The kitchen may be an unlikely place for wooden or papier mâché objects decorated in coloured paper, but this did not prevent manufacturers from creating a plethora of objects to enhance the dinner table or even provide practical assistance for the Highland cook. Oats could be weighed on tartan scales; an egg could be cooked to perfection with the help of a tartan timer and eaten from a tartan egg cup. The examples shown opposite are clad in Prince Charlie tartan, while the tiny salt spoon, only an inch long, must be one of the smallest tartanware items ever made.

Kitchen utensils and equipment naturally have to withstand a high degree of wear and tear, and many of the tartanware objects designed for the cook have not survived as well as other pieces, which were not subject to the same rigorous use. In most cases, tartanware must have been been prized simply as a way of adding colour and interest to an otherwise functional room, and those objects which did not actually have to come into contact with food, and thus end up in the kitchen sink on a regular basis, have lasted well.

Tartanware accessories for dining include napkin rings and candlesticks, sweet dishes and tea caddies, all of which bring a cheerful festivity to the table. For celebrations such as Christmas, Hogmanay or Burn's Night, there can be no more fitting accompaniment to a convivial gathering.

Trays were among the larger items of Mauchline manufacture. The scalloped rectangular example on the left would bring a dash of colour and cheer to a winter's teatime by the fireside. The smaller tray, decorated in Albert tartan (above), has a raised back. In 1850, Smiths were able to boast that their products included 'every article which you can almost conceive it possible to make, from postage stamp boxes up to tea trays'.

Tea, like snuff, needs to be kept dry. As the snuff-box makers looked for ways of diversifying, tea caddies provided an obvious way of expanding their market. Tea containers, featuring the hidden wooden hinge, were among the first articles added to the range of the Ayrshire craftsmen. This double caddy, clad in Stuart tartan, has hinged lids that open to reveal compartments for storing one's favourite blends.

This candlestick, decked in Stuart tartan, would give any Christmas table a festive look. Tartan is now an intrinsic part of the seasonal celebrations, appearing on bows and baubles, wrapping paper and table linen; in fact, tartan has become so much a feature of Christmas that one might be forgiven for thinking that the Nativity took place in a Highland croft rather than a Bethlehem stable. But the simple explanation for tartan's association with Yuletide must be the prevalence of the Christmas colours, red and green, in tartan patterns.

Napkin rings are the most common of all tartanware objects. Manufactured in large quantities and often in numbered sets, they are now the cheapest tartanware items for collectors and the easiest to find. Napkin rings were almost always made of sycamore, which ages to a wonderful golden colour, as demonstrated by the inner surface of these rings. They were made in a variety of widths and generally feature the name of the tartan printed on the side. This selection, from the bottom of the pile up, comprises the princely Stuart, the bold red, green and blue Robertson, the MacFarlane, a black and white check, the ever-popular Prince Charlie, and the distinctive yellow and black McCleod, each graphically offset by black-painted rims.

The splendid chest on the left is a fine example of commissioned tartanware. The lid of the chest opens to reveal four separate tea caddies and two glass mixing bowls in the central compartment. The plinth-style base, decorated with beading, ends in four curved legs on castors for easy movement from place to place. The decoration is actually hand-painted and probably features the tartan of the family for whom it was made. A silver emblem on the lid displays the original owner's crest, now rendered indecipherable by years of polishing.

This miniature tartanware trophy is as handsome as any silver cup. The urn itself is decorated in Macbeth tartan, while the sides of the base are framed in green and red check. A small drawer is fitted in the plinth – the perfect place for keeping a medal won at the Highland Games! For the less athletically-inclined, the urn could simply be set on the sideboard and filled with sweets.

How better to enjoy a nip of the rarest malt than by sipping your Laphroaig, Macallan or Glenlivet from a tartan cup? The beaker above is decorated with a transfer of a Highland scene. More practical perhaps, for the connoisseur of fine whisky, would be the glass on the right, safely stowed in its tartan beaker holder.

ALL BOXED UP

Without the snuff box, there would probably never have been a tartanware industry at all: snuff boxes were the foundation of the Ayrshire trade for nearly thirty years. The characteristic decorated snuff box, with a painted lid featuring Scottish scenes and tartan sides, all hand-executed, has become a collector's piece and commands substantial sums in antique shops and auction houses. Each box is a work of art in itself, which is not surprising since some extremely able artists were engaged to create the designs. Queen Victoria was an avid collector of these beautifully crafted pieces, and was a customer of Smiths, the leading firm in the field.

A box is probably one of the few objects that can be marketed without a specific purpose and, when snuffing went out of fashion, the obvious course for manufacturers was to make boxes in a variety of sizes and shapes to suit whatever needs the customer might have. Boxes designed for more specific requirements were also manufactured and, in the beginning, these tended to be associated with the sort of pastimes men traditionally enjoy. Boxes for cigars, cards and dice were tailored to appeal to the gentleman at leisure.

A cosy gathering of the clans, the large tartanware box shown opposite, with its accompanying ten little boxes, each with its own clan insignia, comes from the top of the tartan-ware range.

A box barely two inches tall has only a limited usefulness. This bibliophile's delight, designed to hold matches, would be perfectly at home on the living-room mantelpiece. An unusual feature is the leather segment applied to the spine. In the days before light and heat could be summoned up by the flick of a switch, the match holder was a common sight by every fireside in the house. Some of these had lids, but most were open containers. Typically, a striking pad was concealed on the underside.

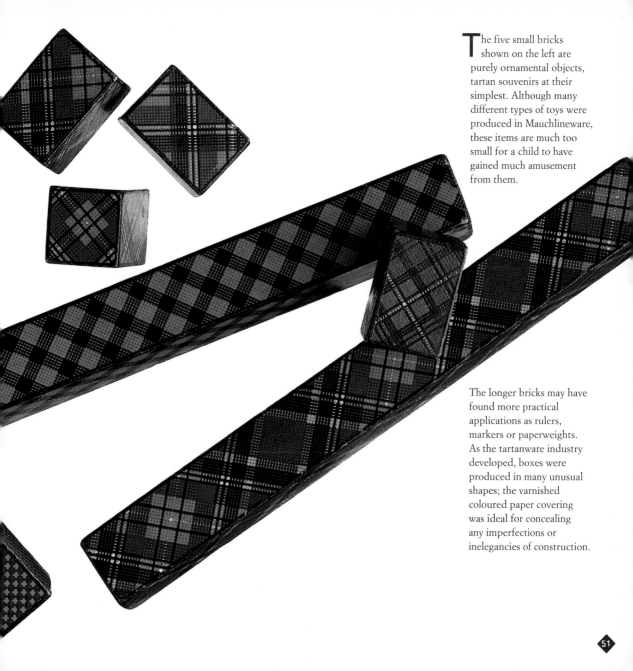

The five small bricks shown on the left are purely ornamental objects, tartan souvenirs at their simplest. Although many different types of toys were produced in Mauchlineware, these items are much too small for a child to have gained much amusement from them.

The longer bricks may have found more practical applications as rulers, markers or paperweights. As the tartanware industry developed, boxes were produced in many unusual shapes; the varnished coloured paper covering was ideal for concealing any imperfections or inelegancies of construction.

V isiting card holders, those indispensable accessories of society life, were also produced in tartanware. The example in the foreground has a hinged lid and the Macbeth tartan covering is embellished with a transfer depicting a shepherd boy and his dogs. Like most tartans, most tartanware features red, green or blue in various combinations; yellow pieces are particularly rare. The first card holder, displaying the Dress McPherson tartan, is a prized find and may have been intended to accompany formal wear; the second features the Buchanan. Many early pieces incorporated positional devices, such as gold stars, to ensure the lids of containers could be replaced the right way round with the tartan properly aligned.

The large box at the base of the pile, with its exposed sycamore edge, represents a unusual hybrid of tartanware and Mauchlineware. The tartan decoration is McFarlane. More typical is the piece resting on top, a tiny box featuring the Frazer tartan, probably designed as a container for buttons or studs. The two cylindrical pieces at the very top of the stack, both sporting the McPherson tartan, may have served as containers for toothpicks or matchsticks, while the cigar-shaped object, clad in Prince Charlie tartan, splits in the middle to reveal a compartment for pen nibs.

This selection of round tartanware boxes features transfer decoration signalling the purpose of each container: no prizes for guessing which of the three held stamps. The boxes with transfers of playing cards were evidently intended as containers for games counters; they are too shallow for holding dice. The representation of tartans varies on many tartanware pieces. Although some clans do have numerous tartans, corresponding to different usages or different family branches, many of the variations seen in tartans of the same name on tartanware objects are probably the result of artistic licence on the part of the manufacturers.

Boxes for storing playing cards comprise another common type of tartanware, reflecting a popular nineteenth-century pastime. The purpose of the containers is usually signalled by the transfer decoration of cards. This book-shaped box, clad in Prince Charlie tartan, holds two decks. The top segment of the 'book', attached to the lid, slides out to open the box.

A STUDY IN TARTAN

The Victorian household comprised a number of distinct domains. Unlike our open-plan, multi-purpose interiors, the typical nineteenth-century house at the upper echelons of society was subdivided into many different rooms, each with its own designated function and pattern of use. Segregation of the sexes was common. Ladies presided over the genteel conversation in the drawing room, or could retreat to the morning room to pursue quieter activities. Gentlemen sought refuge in the male enclaves of the study or library.

The library, as its name suggests, originated as a place for reading and storing books. By the nineteenth century, it had become a kind of unofficial drawing room, where the family might gather on a long winter's evening to huddle round the fire and play games, write letters or read aloud. But the library never quite lost its masculine identity and was always decorated and furnished accordingly.

Tartanware seems particularly at home in this cosy world, where flames leap in the hearth and gilt bindings glint in the murky recesses of tall bookcases. The association of tartan with all the robust outdoor pursuits of Highland life lent a particular character to this evocative retreat.

There are few easier ways of conveying the contents or origin of a book than to clad it in tartan. The works of great Scottish writers such as Robert Burns and Sir Walter Scott enjoyed a tremendous popularity during the nineteenth century. Queen Victoria herself was a devotee of Scott; *The Lay of the Last Minstrel*, which she read with Albert during their first Highland visit, echoed their own rapturous delight in the Scottish scene. This sumptuous box would have been the prize of anyone's library. Clad in the exceptionally rare Lorne tartan, it contains a set of Scottish classics, including *Lord of the Isles*, *Lady of the Lake*, *The Lay of the Last Minstrel* and *Rokeby*. The books are covered in a range of tartans, notably McDuff, Louise and Forty-Second, and the box itself is lined with blue velvet.

For albums or substantial volumes bound in leather or between wooden covers, tartan made an ideal form of decoration. Photography was in its infancy in Victorian times and photograph albums were exciting novelties. The Macbeth album on the right was made for French export: France was a significant market for Mauchlineware pieces. Mother-of-pearl rests on the front and back covers allow the book to be opened flat without damaging the tartan decoration. The album on which it rests is secured with a brass strap-clamp and features the McFarlane tartan in combination with a leather binding. The little notepad in the foreground is ornately decorated; its size and delicacy suggest that it would have been the property of a lady. Equally refined, the tiny McFarlane book (left), only one inch wide by three inches high, must be one of the smallest editions of the Book of Common Prayer ever made. With the help of a magnifying glass every one of its 672 pages is readable.

Tartanware accessories for the desk ranged from pencils to rulers, bookmarks to inkwells – everything for the dedicated correspondent. Books in Victorian times were generally sold with uncut pages and the paper knife, page cutter or letter opener was an important item to have on hand in the study. Since their blades are far from razor-sharp, the examples shown here might equally have served as page folders. The item resting aslant the beautifully shaped Hay and Leith page cutter (below left) is a bookmark clad in Stuart tartan; the Stuart container with rounded ends (below right) is a pen tray. With no telephones or fax machines, but with the benefit of several postal deliveries a day in major towns, letter writing was both an essential and efficient means of communication.

Desk blotters were a feature of every writing table in Victorian times. The McPherson blotter on the left, with its scalloped ends, was made in the late nineteenth century. The knob on top unscrews, enabling the plate to be separated from the curved blotter and a fresh sheet of blotting paper inserted. The Maclean blotter in the foreground dates from

tartanware's twilight years at the beginning of the twentieth century. The design is heavier and less refined and the decoration considerably less precise. The fourteen-sided inkwell decked in the McDuff tartan would make the perfect complement to other tartanware desk accessories.

Cigar cases were among the earliest forms of tartanware products. Both of the examples shown here display exquisitely rendered hunting and fishing scenes bordered by gilt rococo frames and set off by tartan decoration. The artists engaged to paint such charming vignettes were often extremely skilled and the overall workmanship that went into these early pieces attained the highest standards. Like the snuff boxes which predated them, these beautiful objects proved too expensive for the general public and production was discontinued when mechanized techniques were developed.

TARTAN FOR A LADY

For most people, Highland costume means the familiar clansman's kilt, the battledress of gallant Scottish regiments. Highland women, however, also had their traditional tartan garb, notably the arisaid, a length of tartan worn pleated and belted in the manner of the old Highland feileadh. During the nineteenth century, tartan in the form of sashes, shawls, petticoats, ribbons and other trimmings was a regular feature of everyday wear, and it was not only Scotswomen, but also their sisters in the south, who found the effect charming and cheerful. Queen Victoria, who did so much to establish the popularity of tartan outside the Highlands, often wore a tartan sash.

Tartan was high fashion in the late nineteenth century. A Victorian lady could surround herself with mementoes of a pleasant sojourn in the Highlands, with a wealth of tartanware objects. There were tartan-clad manicure sets and fans, tartanware parasol handles and glove stretchers, innumerable containers for personal accoutrements such as hat pins, powder puffs and hair clips, together with other decorative items for the dressing table, from photograph frames to simple boxes and dishes. Tartanware brooches and pins made attractive embellishments for shawls and frocks, while a tartanware handbag must be counted as the ideal accessory for an evening of reeling at a northern meeting.

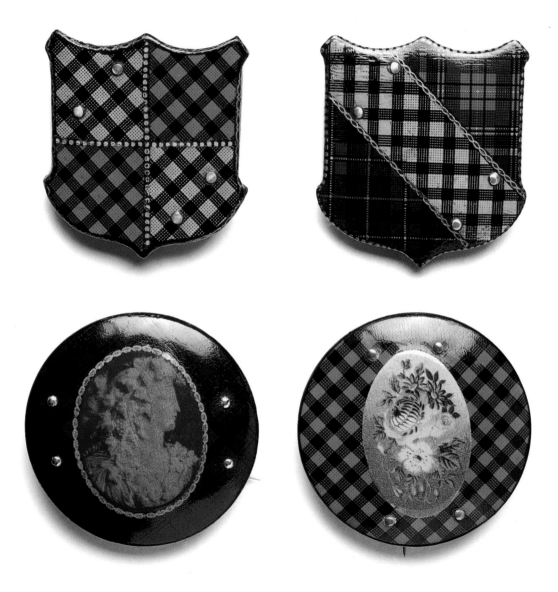

The ultimate in tartan decoration was a piece of tartanware jewellery. These magnificent brooches (left) were ideal for securing a tartan sash at the shoulder and were sported by many a lady at a Highland ball or northern meeting. The shield style was extremely popular and could be worn by either sex. The quartered shield displays a graphic contrast between the red and black Rob Roy and the simple black and white 'Shepherd's' check. Ornaments exclusively for ladies featured more feminine decoration. The bell-shaped object (right) is a 'go-to-bed'. Decorated in the McFarlane tartan, the top separates from the base to reveal a container for matches. A match would be struck on the striking pad under the base and inserted in the little ivory or bone knob at the top of the handle. The lady of the house would then be able to light her way from dressing table to bed without scorching her fingers. Once safely ensconced under the covers, she could be confident that the match would burn out quickly without setting fire to the room. Such objects could also be used for melting sealing wax.

A tartanware occasional table might be considered a little excessive as a holiday souvenir. In fact, the majority of the larger tartanware pieces were commissioned items. Tartanware furniture is rare and expensive. This rococo-style table displays a highly effective use of two tartans, a bold large-scale pattern on the moulding around the circumference and a much smaller check on the legs.

This charming piece with its domed glass cover is a watch holder. A fob watch would have been removed from its chain, hung on a hook over the circular tartan frame and the cover replaced to keep the precious timepiece dust-free.

Tartan was an obvious choice of decoration for wooden photograph frames; indeed, similar articles are still produced today, although these generally employ a fabric rather than a paper covering. The frame on the right is decorated with the Prince Charlie tartan and surrounds an original portrait of a Victorian child. The frame on the left is clad in McPherson tartan.

Tartan is one of the most captivating forms of decoration in the world. The vibrancy of colour and the graphic simplicity of the chequered pattern in all its variations exerts a perennial appeal. These delightful bracelets would have provided yet another opportunity for the tartan enthusiast to display her affection for all things Scottish. Made of tartan-clad wooden segments, threaded together to form a band, these Highland curios often incorporated hand-painted scenes and would probably have been fairly expensive, even at the time.

ACKNOWLEDGEMENTS

I would like to thank all those who have made this book possible, especially Andrew Nicolls, Ian Skelton, Bernard Higton, Noel Gibson, Alex Wilson, Samantha Todhunter, Ted Wilson, Vanessa Holland, the team at Ed Victor's and everyone at Pavilion Books. I am also grateful to the Mauchlineware Collectors Club and Stuart Brownlee at the Cumnock and Doon Valley District Library for all their help.

Also thanks to the following photographers and organizations for their kind permission to reproduce photographs in this book:

The Bridgeman Art Library: pp. 13, 14, 16, 17, 18, 20
Mary Evans Picture Library: p. 11
The Royal Collection © 1996 Her Majesty The Queen: pp. 21, 23